Combating the
Jezebel
Spirit

A Guide to Recognizing and Defeating
the Jezebel Spirit

By
Minister Michael Johnson

Copyright ©2021 Minister Michael Johnson

All rights reserved. No part of this publication may be reproduced, distributed, or transmitted in any form or by any means, including photocopying, recording, or other electronic or mechanical methods, without the prior written permission of the publisher, except in the case of brief quotations embodied in critical reviews and certain other noncommercial uses permitted by copyright law.

Scriptures taken from the Holy Bible, New International Version®, NIV®. Copyright © 1973, 1978, 1984, 2011 by Biblica, Inc.™ Used by permission of Zondervan. All rights reserved worldwide. www.zondervan.com The "NIV" and "New International Version" are trademarks registered in the United States Patent and Trademark Office by Biblica, Inc.™

ISBN: 978-1-951300-21-0

Liberation's Publishing – West Point - Mississippi

Combating the Jezebel *Spirit*

A Guide to Recognizing and Defeating the Jezebel Spirit

Introduction

This book is being written to help individuals recognize and defeat the Jezebel spirit. I was inspired to write this book after recognizing the impact this spirit has in current times and the conflict and deviance that it has caused all throughout history. On a personal note, I was motivated to write this book due to my own conflicts with the spirit of Jezebel. I have experienced firsthand the conflict, negative consequences, and devastation that occur in the aftermath.

I have presented my findings in a way that will teach and capture the reader's attention, so that he or she may be fully invested in the direction and completion of this story. I will introduce to you the story of Barak and Mustang, two individuals who loved each other, yet managed to become entangled with the Jezebel spirit.

The background of each person's story is important. Each moment in their story that made room for this spirit to enter in will be given, followed by identifying traits and tricks it presented to infiltrate the relationship.

The characters in this book are fictional but the stories told are compilations of real-life encounters with this spirit. It is my hope and prayer that God blesses you as you read and learn how to recognize, stop, and rebuke the spirit of Jezebel.

Combating the Jezebel Spirit

Table of Content

Introduction v
Seeking Help 9
Virtual Visits 13
The Entrapment 17
The Confusion 21
What Meant to Kill 29
Salvation 33
Recognizing the Signs 37
    Haughty Titles 38
    Weaponizing Beauty and Sex 39
    Manipulation 40
    Failed Fruit and Controversy 41
    Always Righteous 42
    Baal 43
    Opposition to God's True People 44
    Lies 45
    Unisex 46
Defeating the Jezebel Spirit 47
Conclusion 49

Seeking Help

Barak is a married father of four living in Virginia. He has been married to his wife, Mustang, for almost two decades. They enjoy an above average life, are highly educated, and make well over six-figures. The couple is spiritually saved and have raised their children to be well behaved. They all appear as a successful, well-kept Black family. However, for the past two years, Barak and Mustang have been having problems.

It all began as general marital problems that one would expect a long-lasting couple to have. Yet, their disagreements started to become more frequent and increasingly uncompromising. One disagreement was money. Both of their schedules were busy. They had stopped making time for each other. More and more time seem to pass before they sat down together. Each one's individuality had taken priority over the marriage itself.

Complicating things even more was Barak's struggle with his call to ministry. He had known all of his life that it was what God wanted him to do. From a young age, God spoke to him through dreams. The dreams were extremely frequent as a youth but became less frequent as he became older and his life complicated and tarnished by sin.

So sure was his calling that complete strangers

would approach him in the street and ask him if he was a pastor or if he would pray or help them. Pastors would pull him to the side and tell him he that he had a calling on his life. Barak struggled to believe the validity of it all. He could not fathom why God would choose him, being that in his younger days he was a womanizer. His random sexual encounters with women were often. The acts that earned him his womanizing title were too numerous to remember.

He did not know his Bible as he should, despite always attending church. He had his personal vices as all of us do and like Moses in the Bible, he doubted his ability to complete whatever task God had for him. Now, we all know that God has a knack for intervening when He decides time is time. Barak was at a low place in his life due to the conflict in his home.

He was attending church; he was praying. He was worshipping and praising God, but he could not seem to achieve his goals. He knew deep inside that his prayers and desires could not manifest themselves, because his commitment to God was not being honored. He was not where he needed to be. In an attempt to ease his burden Barak finally decided it was time to accept the calling he knew he had.

His conflict with his calling grew worse, being that he accepted his calling during the same time he was contemplating a divorce. He was confused. How could he be answering a call when the bible's view on divorce is that God hates it? How could one contemplate divorce and be a called man? He decided to reach out to several men and women of the cloth that he had known since birth for pastoral and spiritual counseling.

One of the people he reached out to was Deborah. Deborah was a married mother of three living in Georgia. He knew Deborah from childhood but had not spoken or seen her in several years. He had been traveling all over the world, while she had never traveled outside of the county they grew up in. He was surprised to learn that she was an evangelist and had been ordained as a minister for a few years.

Since he had an attachment to her from childhood coupled with the fact that she was now an ordained minister it was easy for him to allow her to counsel him. He felt comfortable with her. It was entertaining to reminisce about people and events they had mutual knowledge of. What made him most comfortable was her testimony.

While catching him up on her life, Deborah told of how some of her children were fathered by her biological brother whom she had seduced when she was just fourteen. She admitted to having a sexual relationship with him that led to marriage due to her being pregnant. She was young and foolish. She explained how she was sexually immoral. That sexual immorality contributed to a downward spiral in her younger days. She had had affairs with married men.

One affair even lasted four years. She had dropped out of school due to her missing too many days. Skipping school to have sex with multiple men was the norm for her. She had been an alcoholic who once dabbled in a same sex relationship.

However, through God, Deborah reported she had found redemption. She had dedicated her life to God and had been married for a few decades at the time. She was a preacher, evangelist, prophet, and author. Her life was a complete turnaround.

Barak felt validated in his own guilt over his past. This validation he credited to his new relationship with Deborah. He thought he was safe, and there was no way he could have predicted the drama, pain, indecency, and ungodliness that would result from this relationship.

Virtual Visits

Barak and Deborah started to reconnect. It felt good to him to finally feel connected to someone. Every once in a while, Facebook posts turned into text messages and phone calls. Suddenly Deborah was asking him to call her every day; he did. Why wouldn't he? He was not doing anything wrong. There were no red flags that he was conscious of. He was just a man confiding in a woman of God. He even shared the good news with his wife of having a spiritual advisor. This would all change when the helper would become the helpless.

One day, Deborah texted Barak and asked if he could call her as soon as possible. He immediately left his desk at work, walked to his truck in the parking garage and called her. When she answered the phone, she was crying in pain. She went on to explain how she had caught her husband with another woman in the supermarket. Barak did what any good friend would do, and he listened.

During the course of the call, she stated that she needed to be honest about her marriage. She went on to say it had not been going well for a number of years. She went on to say how she had been physically abused by her husband. Barak continued to listen only to find out that her husband was a drug abuser; and that he beat her from time to time with his actual fists.

She reported she had to endure the laughs, stares, and gossip around town because her husband cheats on her openly. Finally, she confessed that she had had numerous affairs over the course of her marriage.

As Barak continued to listen, he began to feel sorry for Deborah. He had grown quite fond of her and immediately wondered why was this woman of God, whom he found to be so powerful and so deserving, has to endure this life of hers?

The call ended and Barak thought of Deborah for the rest of the day on into the night. His conscious began to bother him. He became aware of the possible inappropriateness of his and Deborah's relationship. He stopped texting, messaging, posting, answering, or placing calls to her. After a few days, she contacted him. It was through an unrecognized number. She pleaded to him to talk to her. She told him that she was on assignment from God, and that he needed to hear what she had to say.

He finally called Deborah. She explained that God had given her a prophecy over his life. He asked what it was, and she said she could not give it before he answered a question. She asked him what his cologne smelled like. Barak answered lavender. Deborah then stated that she knew her prophecy was true because she smells lavender whenever God speaks to her. She goes on to tell Barak that God had told her that he was meant to be her husband, and that she was meant to be his wife. Deborah stated that God had reconnected them after all these years because they were soulmates. This was their chance to have what they've always wanted.

Barak was confused by this. He did not know everything about God, but he knew that God did not believe in adultery. He asked Deborah how this could be since adultery is not something God condones. Deborah stated that because they would have true love that God would bless them. She stated that she was not really married. She had a ceremony. They lived as husband and wife, but she and her husband were not legally married.

She goes on to entrap him farther by asking if he believed in the relationship she had with God. She told him about instances when God had given her prophecy to relay to someone, and the consequences God bestowed upon the individual when they did not trust the relationship she had with God.

Barak still was not convinced. However, he did not question her relationship with God. He did not go all in, but he did agree to finally travel to see her face to face. Deborah was speaking at an event and invited Barak to be her special guest. He told Mustang about it, and she supported his travel. He had never asked to do anything like this before. A month later he packed up his fancy truck and made the drive to Deborah. What occurred next could not have been predicted by anyone.

Combating the Jezebel Spirit

The Entrapment

Barak had finally arrived at his destination. After all the calls, messages, facetimes, and emails, he was finally breathing the same air as Deborah. He had planned to stay with a family member. Due to Deborah's prophecy, he did not want to place himself in a compromising position during his visit. He decided a hotel would be compromising. He knew he would not have an opportunity for foul play under the roof of a family member. He called Deborah immediately upon arriving in town.

He expected her to be more ecstatic about seeing him. Instead, she stated that she would not see him until the next day. He thought this was odd, I mean, they had waited for this moment for so long. They were both free to do whatever they wanted right? In the end, he trusted this woman of God and agreed to see her the next day.

Everyone was so happy to see him. He had not been in that place for several years. Folks around town asked him over and over why he had finally come back. He explained he was there to support a friend. They had seen the Facebook posts and inquiring minds wanted to know. What he did not expect was the looks he was receiving from some folk. He repeatedly asked what all the concern was about. His childhood friends, his classmates, and relatives all had something negative to report.

They were concerned that Barak was entertaining Deborah. He could not understand what the concern was about. He had been around women before and in this case, he was spending time with a religious figure. Due to the respect people had for him, these instances never went any farther than concerns. No one directly expressed their concern. As the event approached, Barak was happy to be back in town, and looked forward to the religious experience.

The day of the big event finally came. Barak arrived at the church, looking as good as he always did, and the sanctuary was packed to the max. Not one pew was empty. Speaker after speaker spoke and the attendees seemed to be in the presence of God. Finally, it was Deborah's turn; she was the headliner. She gave a personal testimony of things that had occurred in her life, and how God had brought her over. She told of her sexually immoral past and even come clean about her bad marriage. The congregation cheered and rose to their feet as she exclaimed that this day was the day she was breaking her chains. God had her exactly where she needed to be. She even asked Barak to stand and expressed to everyone how much she loved him and thanked him for helping her break free.

Barak had never felt so appreciated. Here he was just coming to support a friend and Deborah had shined the spotlight on him. He did not know what to do. He was not used to that treatment due to the issues in his own marriage. After the event Barak stayed behind to help Deborah. She explained she had a surprise for him, but he had to agree to ask no questions. Barak agreed and off they went.

Deborah took Barak to a hotel. As soon as she closed the door, she had her clothes off. He was so hesitant. This is not where he wanted to be. This was not the intentions he had for their relationship. He also was not sexually attracted to Deborah. He was a man who never had any issue with the opposite sex, and Deborah was physically not his type. She was overweight, not curvy as he liked. Her body appeared worn and used. Her breasts were empty, and her stretch marks were not badges of childbearing. She had been put down fast and ridden hard so to speak. Barak asked how could this not be wrong? Deborah told Barak it was not. Deborah stated that God had sanctioned this because it was his will. Barak eventually was naked, on top of her, kissing her, but he could not perform. He eventually cried, right on top of her, because he was so embarrassed. He just could not bring himself to do this. He was after all a married man and Deborah had not aroused him sexually. He told her he was nervous, blamed it on being tired and could not. Deborah said it was okay and asked if he could just hold her. He agreed to do so.

He held her on this night and they both slept. She appeared to be sad because tomorrow he was travelling back home, halfway across the nation. She told Barak that she was sure now that God was giving Barak to her. She revealed that God had told her of all the wondrous and abundant things they would have and accomplish as one. Barak took all of this in. Barak and Deborah left the hotel. Deborah asked if he would kiss her. Barak kissed Deborah, bid her goodbye, and traveled back home.

The Confusion

Back home, Barak was a man conflicted. He had decided his marriage was over. That time away sealed that fate. He was still unsure about his relationship with Deborah. They continued to call each other and speak day and night. They would email back and forth even making plans to see each other again. Mustang knew something was not right. She questioned Barak about his relationship with Deborah. Barak did not deny anything was going on. Why should he? His marriage was all but over. This triangle of people created more tension and chaos in the home. This led to Barak eventually moving out of the family home across country where Deborah was.

Back in Georgia, Barak felt everything was falling into place. He felt hurt, sadness and disappointment over leaving his family behind. He reasoned that the fighting was so frequent and explosive it was not best for the children. He, in fact, had come from broken homes. He lived with the same father but had four stepmothers between the ages of eight and fifteen. He also did not have a relationship with his own mother who left his life at the age of four. His home life as a youth was filled with women in and out the door. There also was a convoluted relationship with a woman who frequented his father's bed while having a husband and children across town. Barak felt he was doing the best thing for his children by eliminating the arguments and combativeness of their home.

Barak was staying with his father again, which was a difficult pill to swallow. However, it gave him an outlet to see Deborah more and more as she lived only a few minutes away. Things did not go as expected. Deborah was unavailable most of the time, and only met Barak at night at the park. It was during this time that Barak first met Deborah's youngest child, Tyrone, a son eleven years of age. Deborah's son appeared to have mental health issues often acting out in a manner not acceptable for a three-year-old, let alone an eleven-year-old.

Tyrone was extremely clingy. Tyrone would interrupt Deborah if she was giving anyone attention other than him. He would exhibit inappropriate behavior such as passing gas, burping, cursing and even displaying violent behavior. Tyrone had been held back in school so many times, he was only in the third grade.

One night, he, Deborah and Tyrone were spending time together. All of a sudden Tyrone started screaming, crying, and yelling inaudible words. Deborah attempted to calm him down by coddling him as you would do a toddler, but nothing worked. Tyrone started acting this way after Barak attempted to leave for the night. Barak was confused and did not know what to do. Deborah was yelling at him because she did not want him to leave. She was upset that he had upset the child.

Deborah explained that Tyrone did have mental health issues and did not face rejection well due to the men that had left them before. Barak was not aware of anyone, let alone, men in a plural sense. "How many had there been?" He thought to himself. "What frequency was there? What else did he not know?" After Barak asked these questions, Deborah lashed out at him and told him to go back home to Virginia and never return. Barak immediately retrieved his things from his father home and traveled towards home.

He immediately called Mustang and revealed something he had been feeling but had not disclosed before. He felt Deborah had some sort of hold on him. Again, she was not his type. He had never been involved or pursued a woman of her lack of class before. He wanted to be with his family, but there was something inside of him that was fighting against his better judgement. He asked Mustang to not consider him crazy, but that night on the phone while he was driving, he told her he felt as if this situation was a spiritual one. He felt as if something he was not prepared for was intervening in his life. He felt that Deborah could possibly be something that could not be recognized by flesh and only in spirit.

Back home in Virginia, Barak was reunited with his family. He blocked all communication with Deborah. She couldn't reach him by cell phone or email. Barak was dedicated to reestablishing himself with his family. He was taking the time to reinvest himself at home. Everything seemingly was falling back into place. That is, until Barak started receiving phone calls from a number he had not seen before. Barak immediately felt he knew who it was and blocked this number immediately. He did not want any contact with Deborah.

One night, while lying in bed, Barak had an awful feeling. He felt something was off, but he did not know what it was. He began scrolling through his phone. He received a spam email. Upon opening it, he realized it was a message from Deborah. They had not spoken in over a month; why was she contacting him? Intrigued, he read the message and he quickly realized it was a suicide note.

She said how she was currently overindulging on wine and prescription medication. She stated she had been doing so for a few hours. The message stated she did not want to go on without him. She was so heartbroken that she decided to take her life. She had written goodbyes to Tyrone, her husband and even him.

Barak immediately woke Mustang and informed her of what was happening. Even though, he did not want anything to do with Deborah, he was concerned. He asked Mustang if he could call. He agreed to put the phone on speaker so Mustang could listen.

During the call, Deborah stated that she loved Barak so much. She stated that she was choosing to kill herself rather than fail God. When asked how she was failing God. She stated God had told her she and Barak were meant to be and that their union was important to the Kingdom of God. Deborah was committed to killing herself on this night. Barak stated he was contacting local law enforcement to get her some assistance. He did not want her to kill herself. Deborah begged him to not contact anyone and stated she would stop if he agreed to come see her. Mustang told Barak to go; she also did not wish for anyone, even Deborah, to commit suicide. Barak gathered his things and went to Georgia once again.

After arriving Barak found himself in this familiar position again. He was lying there on the bed naked. His clothes were off and Deborah on top of him. She was doing everything in her ability to arouse him, but he could not perform. She was enjoying the moment on top of him enjoying herself, as he was lying there going through the motions. It didn't feel right. "What is going on here? He thought. He had never had this issue before. He had been with many women and was always ready to go. These moments with her he never was. He was attracted to Mustang back home and immediately did not have this issue. "So why was he having the issue with Deborah?" He thought.

Afterwards, as she lay there sleep and satisfied, he really began to think about this situation. He knew the issue was happening because he did not want to be there so why was he? He woke Deborah up and stated that he wanted this to be over. He explained to her that he loved Mustang and he could not see a future between them.

Deborah lunged at Barak. He was grabbing at her to move her away, but she had her hands around his throat. He fell back on the bed, and she was straddling him and choking him. He was not going to hit a woman, but the choking was becoming intense. He used force and restrained her by holding her wrists. He explained to her that a Woman of God should not be violent like this. Barak called the police to show Deborah he was serious about wanting her out of his space and out of his life. She packed her things and told Barak God was going to punish him for shunning her. She even told Barak that he was going to die for not trusting God and not being with her.

She left before the police arrived. Barak had choke marks all around his neck. He declined to press charges and the officer informed him he had one year to do so. Barak called Deborah and informed her of what he had done. He wanted to make clear to her that he was finished and wanted no part of her foolishness. Deborah could not hear Barak. The only thing she was concerned with was if the police was coming to her home or not. She informed Barak that her husband was going to "beat her ass" if he found out she was with another man.

This floored Barak. He noticed the concern Deborah had over her husband and he immediately knew she had been lying about her husband the entire time. Barak hung up on Deborah but not before she could tell him that nothing would go right in his life and that God would bring him back.

Combating the Jezebel Spirit

What Meant to Kill

Once again, Barak was home in Virginia. The relationship between he and Mustang was deteriorating faster than ever. Mustang was accusing Barak of continuing a relationship with Deborah daily. Although he was not speaking to Deborah, Mustang was sure he was and was growing angrier by the day.

Unknown to Barak, Deborah started contacting Mustang. Deborah had built a bond with Mustang. Deborah had convinced Mustang that Barak had been pursuing her, and they both were women being used and manipulated by the same man. Deborah told Mustang that Barak had been pursuing her for a year, and she had been declining his advances. Deborah presented herself as a comforter and supporter of Mustang. Deborah would call Mustang daily in secret and give her so called updates about Barak. All of these efforts were making Mustang more upset and angrier at Barak. The arguments in their home increased in frequency and intensity. Barak was telling Mustang he had not had any contact with Deborah. She would not believe him.

Deborah grew angrier and angrier with Barak. She was mad beyond anything she had ever experienced before. Barak started receiving messages from Deborah. He ignored her efforts. In a desperate attempt she began to reach out to him through mutual acquaintances of theirs. Barak grew frustrated and eventually wanted to make it clear to Deborah that he was not going to speak with her and that she should quit her efforts. He agreed to speak to her and during the conversation; Deborah stated that God had told her that Mustang would attempt to kill him. She stated that God had told her this over a few dreams and conversations with God.

At that moment, Mustang burst into the room. She yelled that she had caught Barak pursuing Deborah. She was listening in on the call with Deborah on three-way. Barak explained that it was not what it seemed. Deborah had Mustang listen in at some points in the conversation and muted her during others. Mustang went into a fit of rage. She was tired of Barak's lying and her heart had been broken all over again. Mustang thanked Deborah for exposing the truth to her and on this day Barak and Mustang agreed to separate. However, not everything is what it appears to be. Deborah's manipulation was not over yet.

Before Barak could even get down the street with his belongings, Deborah was calling him. She asked him if he now saw that God wanted her and him to be together. Her prophecies were coming true. Barak was unaware of the manipulation and began to acknowledge the validity of Deborah's advances. He agreed to give their relationship another try.

Back in Georgia, Deborah felt she finally had gotten her man. Unknown to any of the major people in this story, Deborah had been living with her husband Jerome and son Tyrone all this time. Now that Barak was separated from Mustang and moving back home, she had to get Jerome out of the picture. With no explanation or warning, she packed Jerome's things while he was at work and placed them on the stoop. She dismissed her own husband as one would dismiss household trash. She was making a bed for Barak now that he was with her again.

With Barak now fully separated from his family and friends, Deborah began to isolate him even more, so his only relationship was with her. She began prophesying daily over his life. She was using God as a manipulation tool. She would email and call him daily to remind him of the purpose God had for him in her life. She would make up stories involving family and friends to make him angry at others and isolate him even more.

Eventually, Barak and Mustang filed for divorce and with the finalization of that divorce only three weeks away, Deborah sprang another wrench. She informed Barak that God had shown her that he had to propose to her in a church in order for God to be happy. Barak had been manipulated into believing whatever Deborah told him, so in front of a church congregation, he did just that. Everyone was so happy and excited about this union, but deep inside Barak was not feeling comfortable. Something was still off, and he did not know what it was.

He was evaluating his life, and he was not sure how he was with a woman like Deborah. His life was now so different from what he had worked so hard to achieve. He was used to fine dining and desired wardrobes, but now he was eating from the bottom of the barrel and taking showers in a rusted tub. Barak began to ask God to fill him with the Holy Spirit so he could have direction. It did not happen the first, second or third time, but the last time he asked at church. On that fourth Sunday, God finally showed up.

Salvation

Barak was in a state of enlightenment. For the first time in his life, he truly felt the presence of God. It was the best feeling he had ever experienced in his life. Simultaneously, he had such an awesome fear of God that he had never had before. Sitting in the pew, on this Sunday, he could not contain what he was feeling. Barak rose from his seat and ran out the back of the church. He found himself in a bathroom alone just God and he, and the tears were flowing like rain.

After church, Barak spent time away from Deborah. He had shared with her what had occurred in his life. He expected joy, celebration, and congratulations from her but instead received what he did not expect. Deborah was extremely critical of what Barak was reporting. She told him to calm down and to not make a big deal of it. She asked him to stop mentioning it, and even told him to not expect her to pat him on the back. Her reasoning was it was his first anointing and compared to her anointing, he was still a rookie.

During this time alone, Barak thought about the events of the previous months. Sitting outside under God's sky, he could finally acknowledge his mistakes in the process and knew he wanted to make things right. After some time, he called Deborah and confessed his actions that could have been done better.

He stated to her that he did not want to upset God any more than he already had. They had to proceed correctly and properly in their relationship.

Deborah did not want to hear what he was saying. She told him that God could not have a better relationship with him than the one she has with God. Deborah told Barak that he needed to trust her despite what God was saying to him. She attempted to persuade him to lean unto her understanding and not his own. Barak, however, stood his ground and stated if they could not continue in a manner acceptable to God he could not continue. Deborah told Barak he was going against God's wishes, and God would punish him. Barak stated he was willing to take that chance, so he could stand in his convictions.

Confused, Barak called Mustang to check on his children and also to issue an apology to her. During the call, Mustang asked him what was wrong. She could sense something was off with him. Barak told her that she did not want to know, but Mustang assured him that she wanted to be there for him. It was here that Barak heard one of the Godliest things he had ever heard in his life. Mustang told him that she wanted to hear what was wrong, because she wanted what was best for Barak even if it was not best for her.

As soon as Barak heard this, he felt immediate regret for the past months or maybe even the past years of their marriage. He recognized the Christianity in what Mustang had said. It floored him and he was in disbelief because the love in those words was too great to ignore. He told Mustang of all that had occurred to him and towards the end of the call, he asked Mustang for her forgiveness. Barak also asked if they could try again and of course, Mustang answered yes.

Barak had a plane ticket to return home. There were a few days before his departure date. He had been reading his Bible every day for months. He also had been watching television shows centered on religious education. For some reason, today's teaching was on the Jezebel spirit. The more he watched, the more he recognized similarities between the Jezebel spirit and his recent circumstances.

Barak was floored. Barak was in a state of disbelief. He had heard of the Jezebel spirit before but had never researched it. He immediately began looking through his Bible to learn the story and to find out anything he could about it. He went to his father and asked if he had ever heard of a Jezebel spirit. Barak's father looked at him in awe and asked why he asked. Barak told him what was on his mind and his father repeatedly asked him why this was on his mind and if Mustang had told him anything about the subject. Barak was confused as to this question but answered no. Barak's father instructed Barak to ask Mustang about the Jezebel spirit.

Barak did not know why he was asked to do this. However, he called Mustang and told her of the conversation between his father and him. Mustang began to cry, and Barak was even more confused. Mustang told Barak that she and his father had been speaking of the Jezebel spirit for months. They recognized the situation for what it was long ago. They had been praying and praying for Barak to be delivered from his ordeal. They did not mention it to him because they were trusting God to intervene.

Recognizing the Signs

Jezebel was a Phoenician princess who married King Ahab in the Book of Kings in the Bible. Shortly after their marriage, the religion of Baal Melqart was imported into the kingdom of Israel. This religion was practiced by the Phoenicians and Baal was recognized as the ruler of the universe of king of the underworld. This was an outrageous violation of the covenant between God and his people, and this action was combated by the prophet Elijah. Jezebel sought to oppose and kill God's prophets in order to promote her agenda.

The pride, greed, selfishness, and lack of fear of God led her to her death. Jezebel had used beauty, sex, manipulation, and influence to gain a seat next to those she wanted to control. The Jezebel spirit is one that is still relevant in our day. Recognizing the traits of a Jezebel spirit is something not easy to do. Here, we will learn of some of those traits and how to combat them.

Haughty Titles

Jezebel will often call her or himself a prophetess, prophet or any haughty title recognized in religious circles. In this story, Deborah called herself an evangelist. She also claimed to have a prophetic relationship with God. Instead of being a true child of God, a Jezebel will serve their own selfish self-interests. Many will open churches or hop around from platform to platform in order to perform in the spotlight. Their religious message is not rooted in the gospel. It is rooted in their interests such as money, sex, prosperity, or harvest.

In the conference Deborah had, she was the star. The conference highlighted her accomplishments and her story. Jesus or God were the accompaniment to her opening act. Throughout her dealings with Barak and many others, her prophecies were greatly beneficial to her and her agenda. Nothing that she relayed as told by God was about anyone other than her.

Weaponizing Beauty and Sex

Jezebel will use beauty and sex as a weapon to promote their purpose. In this story, Barak did not even know what Deborah truly looked like until the end. Deborah would wake up before the light of dawn and enclose herself in a room. It was here that she donned her wig, fake eyelashes, girdle, and a ton of makeup. To capture Barak, Deborah wanted to appear as what he desired. That beauty is an attempt to mask the character of a Jezebel.

Once a fly is entangled in the web, Jezebel uses sex to further ensnare. Deborah was well experienced in sexual practice. Remember, from the early teenage years, Deborah had promoted and engaged in deviant sexual acts. A Jezebel, through multiple and numerous sexual partners, becomes proficient in sexual deeds. Although Deborah presented herself as a Woman of God, it was she who would create the sexual opportunity between Barak and herself. Deborah had the hotel already booked. Deborah was the one who initiated sex. Deborah was the one who always presented sex between Barak and her as a Godly sanctioned act.

Manipulation

Jezebel will use manipulation to their advantage. Throughout Barak and Deborah's journey, Deborah was involved in manipulation of some kind every step along the way. From the beginning, she presented herself as something she was not. Every time Deborah felt she was losing control of Barak, she presented another prophecy or revelation to keep him close.

Deborah even had a fake conference and created situations in order to trap Barak. Later we learned that Deborah was driving those close to Barak away from him in order to leave her as the last person standing; the last person Barak could turn to. Remember, Deborah had told Barak's family that he was pursuing her, and she did not want anything to do with him. Deborah also presented herself as a confidant to Mustang and further drove a wedge in between their marriage. By telling Mustang things about Barak to make her disappointed in him and by giving Barak fake prophecy concerning Mustang, Deborah appeared to know what she was talking about.

Failed Fruit and Controversy

Jezebel will be judged by their fruit. Everything Deborah had been involved in ultimately was surrounded in controversy. She had children by a brother, multiple affairs, and routine sexual deviance in her life. Deborah's own mental health issues had manifested themselves in Tyrone. Despite all the anointing and favor she claimed to have, she could not rise above her actual reality. Everything she touches or is involved in rotten as fruit does. Controversy always follows her because controversy is the reality and truth.

Always Righteous

Jezebel is always righteous. They never do anything wrong and rarely accepts responsibility for anything unless it is a manipulation tactic. Deborah always had the answer. Her plan, her ideas, her purpose was always portrayed by her as being better than anyone else's. She was highly critical of God's people and would often critique religious authority. Once, during a church service, Deborah even spoke with Barak about a church takeover, stating that she could do a better job. Being always right is another tool of control for Jezebel.

Baal

Jezebel serves Baal and opposes God. Baal is the God of prosperity, money, harvest, and sex. Although Deborah appeared as someone who worships God, her agenda targeted those things Baal finds important. Deborah wanted to upgrade her situation. Barak, being educated, well-traveled and accomplished was her path to upgrade. We already know Jezebel is destined to fail but this does not prevent Jezebel from attempting to win. Deborah preached a message of prosperity. She was never satisfied with what she had but always chased where she wanted to go. Any church she was involved in that preached the gospel was not places she felt comfortable. This is why Deborah took Barak to several places of worship. She only felt at home in places where the message was not the gospel but was instead prosperity, harvest, money, and sex.

Opposition to God's True People

Jezebel hates those truly called by God. Remember how all of this began. Barak was accepting a calling. He reached out for assistance. When dealing in the spirit world, spirit recognizes spirit. Deborah attempted throughout this story to prevent Barak from standing before the Lord. She introduced ideas and practices that truly turned him away from God. Deborah was also highly critical of religious authority.

Lies

Jezebel lies. Jezebel lies to create reality. Jezebel lies to mask evildoing. Jezebel lies every time they speak. Deborah did not present herself as who she really was. She lied to make herself more appealing to Barak. It was her lies that created every situation in her life that was not of God. If Deborah was speaking, she was lying. She lied on God, on people and even lied on herself.

Unisex

Jezebel can be a man or a woman. Jezebel is defined by traits not gender. Jezebel can be your wife, husband, sister, brother, father, mother, or anyone. This fact makes some more susceptible to the Jezebel spirit than others because many are raised by a Jezebel. Barak was raised by a Jezebel. Barak's father has been married six times. Barak's father had had an affair with a married woman for years. Throughout Barak's life, his father presented himself as a Man of God. His father was a manipulator, liar, false witness, and this normalized the Jezebel spirit for Barak. He did not recognize it when it appeared in his own life because it was his way of life growing up.

Defeating the Jezebel Spirit

Revelation 2:20-22 New International Version "Nevertheless, I have this against you: You tolerate that woman Jezebel, who calls herself a prophet. By her teaching she misleads my servants into sexual immorality and the eating of food sacrificed to idols, I have given her time to replant of her immorality, but she is unwilling. So, I will cast her on a bed of suffering, and I will make those who commit adultery with her suffer intensely, unless they repent of her ways.

Deborah was not the only one to blame for these events. Barak had a part to play in these events as well. Barak entered into, participated in, and promoted the relationship through a lack of spiritual maturity and religious stability. Proverbs 3:5 teaches that we should not lean unto our own understanding. There is no earthly prophecy or instruction from God that will supersede God's word and promise.

In Revelations 2:22, we are told that those under the influence of a Jezebel must repent of their ways. This involves severing ties with a Jezebel spirit. This is not always so easy. This makes prayer another tool that must be utilized. The individual must pray and specifically ask God to intervene. It also is extremely helpful to pray in agreement with another man or woman of God. Matthew 18:19 tells us that if at least two believers come in agreement and ask God of anything, not only will God be there but He will intervene.

The individual influenced must attempt to live a life pleasing in God's sight after they ask for and repent. James 4:7 states that after we repent and surrender to God, it is only then that we may resist the enemy. It has to be in this order, or it will not work. God cannot bless any mess so the individual must be mess free. All ways, customs and mannerisms that were present, learned or practiced during interaction with a Jezebel spirit must be eliminated. Remember, a Jezebel spirit uses the flesh in order to gain an advantage, but this is truly a battle of the spirit. Barak was not rooted in his relationship with God as he should have been. If he were, he would have recognized the deviance of the situation.

Conclusion

Hopefully, you learned something from the story of Barak, Mustang and Deborah. One thing you must know is that Jezebel is already defeated. Thankfully, we serve a God who is all powerful and available to those who seek Him. These traits are only a few that make up a Jezebel spirit. If confronted with a Jezebel, the only way to combat it is through the love, grace, and mercy of God. Praise God Barak had a Mustang to pray for and cover him.

Today, Barak and Mustang are happily married and actively seeking to be witnesses and ambassadors of God. They never divorced and never plan to.

To God Be the Glory. All Glory to God.

Combating the Jezebel Spirit

www.ingramcontent.com/pod-product-compliance
Lightning Source LLC
Chambersburg PA
CBHW050335120526
44592CB00014B/2200